All the Ligh   ee

by

Anthony Doerr

A 30-minute Instaread Summary

Please Note

This is an unofficial summary. We encourage you to purchase the full book if you have not already. We will give you 10% off up to $1 on the digital version of the full-form book or $1 off on the physical version of the full-form book. Please see last page of this summary for info on how to redeem this discount.

document as a citation or source of information does not imply that the author or publisher endorses the information that the individual or organization provided. This concise summary is unofficial and is not authorized, approved, licensed, or endorsed by the original book's author or publisher.

Contents

Book Overview

Marie-Laure is a young, French girl who lost her sight when she was only six. Her father, a locksmith at the natural history museum in Paris, does his best to help her live a normal life by teaching her to read Braille and making models of their neighborhood so she can learn to get around on her own.

Werner is an orphaned child who lives in an orphanage in Germany with his sister, Jutta. Werner is very intelligent and wants to become a scientist. He teaches himself math and how to repair radios because of his fascination with radio waves. With the radios he has built, Werner and his sister listen to science programs in French. Eventually Werner comes to the attention of a German official who makes it possible for him to attend a proper school. Werner's experiences in school are not ideal, but he learns a great deal about himself and, with the help of a professor, creates a way in which to locate transmissions from illegal radio broadcasts. It is this transceiver he will use and repair during his time as a soldier in the war.

Marie-Laure and her father, Daniel, flee Paris at the beginning of the German occupation and end up in Saint-Malo at her great-uncle, Etienne's, house. The museum gave Daniel a rare diamond, the Sea of Flames, to keep safe, but it is said to be cursed. It will allow the owner to live a long life, but destroy the owner's loved ones. Daniel hides it in a tiny model of Etienne's house, part of a model of the town he built to help Marie-Laure learn to get around the city alone. He gets a telegram ordering him back to Paris, but is arrested and never seen again. Etienne and Marie-Laure begin helping the resistance. She picks up messages hidden in loaves of bread and he broadcasts them.

After a brutal series of missions in Russia and Austria, Werner and his unit go to Saint-Malo to find the transceiver Etienne is using. The allies are pushing through Europe, but Saint-Malo is a last German stronghold on the Atlantic coast. Werner finds Etienne's antenna, but does not turn him in because he recognizes the voice transmitting the resistance messages. It is the radio science professor from his childhood.

During the American bombardment of Saint-Malo, Werner gets trapped in a hotel cellar. After repairing his radio, he hears Marie-Laure broadcasting. He already knows who she is because he tracked the resistance transmitter to Etienne's home and saw her leave the house. Etienne has been arrested and she is alone. She calls for help because there is someone in the house. Werner wants to help her.

Werner's sergeant uses grenades to blow a hole in the debris of the collapsed cellar and Werner rushes to Etienne's house. Marie-Laure is hiding in the attic, where the transceiver is, from an intruder who has tracked the Sea of Flames to the house. The intruder, Sergeant Major Von Rumpel, a Nazi treasure appraiser, is dying of cancer and thinks the diamond could save him.

Werner arrives in time to kill Von Rumpel and save Marie-Laure. They hide together in Etienne's cellar as bombs continue to fall. He learns about her connection to the science professor. Werner thinks he may be in love with Marie-Laure, but he knows she will be safer without him. When the bombing stops, she takes him to her secret place by the sea, a grotto guarded by a gate, where she casts away the tiny house. They part. Marie-Laure is reunited with Etienne, but Werner is captured and dies when he steps on a landmine while delirious from an illness. Several decades later, Werner's sister receives his personal items, which include the tiny model of Etienne's house. She tracks it to Saint-Malo and returns it to Marie-Laure. Inside there is the iron key to her grotto, a gift she made to Werner.

Main Characters

Marie-Laure LeBlanc: Marie-Laure is a Parisian teen who went blind at the age of six.

Daniel LeBlanc: Daniel is Marie-Laure's widowed father who helps her adapt to blindness. He is the key master and locksmith for the natural history museum in Paris.

Werner Pfennig: Werner is a German orphan who attends Schulpforta, a Nazi political school. He works on a key transmitter project as a student, then is pressed into military service as a radio expert during World War II.

Jutta Pfennig: Jutta is Werner's little sister, who loves to draw pictures of an imaginary Paris. She has a strong sense of right and wrong.

Etienne LeBlanc: Etienne is Marie-Laure's great-uncle. He has not left the family home in Saint-Malo since serving in World War I.

Madame Manec: Madame is Etienne's housekeeper. She proves her bravery during World War II by helping the resistance fight against their German occupiers.

Frederick: Frederick is a wealthy student who shares a bunk with Werner at school. He is bullied by other students and eventually suffers brain damage after a severe beating.

Frank Volkheimer: An older student at Schulpforta, Frank is a giant who is ordered to watch out for Werner at school. Later he is Werner's sergeant.

Reinhard von Rumpel: Von Rumpel estimates the value of jewels and hunts for treasures for the Nazis. He spends the war hunting for the Sea of Flames diamond.

Chapter Summaries and Key Happenings

Part Zero

Chapter 1

Just ahead of an American attack, leaflets fall from the sky to warn residents of a city to evacuate.

Key Happenings

- Leaflets fall on a city to warn of an impending U.S. attack.

Chapter 2

Twelve American bombers cross the English Channel.

Key Happenings

- U.S. bombers prepare an attack.

Chapter 3

Marie-Laure LeBlanc sits alone inside her great-uncle Etienne's home in Saint-Malo. She hears planes flying overhead. A flyer warning of an impending assault by American bombers lands near her, but she is blind and cannot read it.

Key Happenings

- Marie-Laure LeBlanc, a blind girl, is alone in her great-uncle's home in Saint-Malo as the allied assault on the city begins.

Chapter 4

Private Werner Pfennig wakes in the Hotel of Bees where his unit is billeted in Saint-Malo. A corporal orders him to go to the cellar. The hotel once was a privateer's lair. It is fortress-like and houses an antiaircraft gun manned by a crew of Austrians.

Key Happenings

- Private Werner Pfennig takes refuge in the cellar of the Hotel of Bees.

Chapter 5

The townspeople who have not evacuated awake to the noise of guns and planes amid the shower of leaflets. In a fortress, the last German bastion on the Breton coast, French prisoners peer up at the sky.

Other sieges have rocked the city of Saint-Malo over the centuries, but none like this.

Key Happenings

- The remaining residents of Saint-Malo take cover as the assault begins.

- The Germans will defend their last stronghold on the Breton coast, a fortress in Saint-Malo.

Chapter 6

Marie-Laure kneels by her model of Saint-Malo as the bombers fly over. She picks up the tiny model of her uncle's house and slides off three panels on the roof to remove a teardrop-shaped stone the size of a pigeon's egg.

Key Happenings

- Instead of going to the cellar, Marie-Laure stays by her miniature city and takes out a large stone hidden in the model of her uncle's home.

Chapter 7

Werner checks his radio in the cellar of the Hotel of Bees. His staff sergeant, Frank Volkheimer, tells him they will be safe there. Their engineer, Bernd, is last to join them. The Austrians keep firing the antiaircraft gun and singing.

Key Happenings

- Werner, Volkheimer and Bernd shelter in the cellar of the Hotel of Bees.

Chapter 8

Marie-Laure's great-uncle, a prisoner at Fort National, watches as the sky turns black and thinks of locusts in the Old Testament. The twelve bombers deliver their payload. Marie-Laure hides under her bed. Werner's cellar refuge goes dark.

Key Happenings

- The twelve American bombers drop their bombs on the city of Saint-Malo.

Part One

Chapter 9

At the age of six, Marie-Laure is going blind. Her father sends her on a tour of natural wonders at the museum where he works. The guide tells the tour group about the Sea of Flames, a rare diamond that is said to be cursed. According to legend, the diamond was a gift from the Goddess of the Earth to her lover the God of the Sea. The stone keeps its owner alive no matter what, but the owner's loved ones are cursed to suffer terrible deaths. The curse can be broken if the stone returns to the sea. The stone belongs to the museum and is kept behind a series of thirteen iron doors.

Marie-Laure loses all her sight within the next month.

Key Happenings

- Marie-Laure goes blind at age six.

- At the museum where her father works, Marie-Laure hears the legend of the Sea of Flames, a rare diamond that is thought to be cursed.

Chapter 10

After the death of their father, Werner and his younger sister, Jutta, live in an orphanage in

Zollverein, a town outside Essen, Germany. They stand out because of their snowy hair. Werner also has an appetite for knowledge while Jutta is an artist. She often draws pictures from images inspired by stories of Paris told to them by Frau Elena, the Protestant nun from Alsace who runs the orphanage. Werner and Jutta often explore the mines in their town, including Pit Nine where their father died.

Key Happenings

- Werner and his little sister, Jutta, live in a small orphanage outside Essen, Germany.

Chapter 11

Marie-Laure's father helps her learn to adjust to her blindness by teaching her to read Braille. He also helps her be more independent by building her a scale model of their neighborhood.

Marie-Laure often accompanies her father to his job as locksmith and key master for the museum. She spends many afternoons with Dr. Geffard, an expert in mollusks. He lets her feel and study all kinds of specimens.

Key Happenings

- Marie-Laure and her father adapt to her blindness. She learns to get around and to read Braille.

- Marie-Laure accompanies her father to his job at the natural history museum. There, she often spends time with Dr. Geffard, an expert in mollusks, who allows her to touch and study many different specimens.

Chapter 12

When Werner is eight, he finds a broken radio and teaches himself how to fix it. He is moved to tears when he hears music on the radio for the first time. He becomes fascinated by radio waves.

Key Happenings

- At eight, Werner learns to fix radios.

Chapter 13

Marie-Laure's father teaches her to solve puzzle boxes. She has studied the neighborhood model but is afraid to rely on it.

Key Happenings

- Marie-Laure is still unable to use her knowledge of the model of her neighborhood to walk it independently.

Chapter 14

Werner harvests old and broken parts to make radios. The children and Frau Elena listen to news, music, and folk shows on them. They hear broadcasts of a play about hook-nosed invaders who plot to murder German children, but the intruders are turned in by a patriotic neighbor.

Key Happenings

- Werner learns more about radios.

- Frau Elena and the children at the orphanage hear Nazi propaganda broadcasts on radios Werner has provided them.

Chapter 15

Marie-Laure uses her knowledge of the neighborhood model her father built for her. She and her father share a moment of joy when she successfully directs them home on a snowy day.

Key Happenings

- Marie-Laure uses the model her father built her to get around her neighborhood successfully.

Chapter 16

Werner is ten. Two boys at the orphanage join the Hitler Youth. Unwilling to follow that path, Werner tries to keep his head down. He studies science and comes up with ideas for inventions such as X-ray goggles.

An official comes to the orphanage to praise Hitler. He tells the boys they will work for Germany in the mines. Werner feels trapped.

Key Happenings

- Werner teaches himself science, but realizes his fate lies in the mines.

Chapter 17

Marie-Laure can navigate the museum using smells, sounds, pipes, cables, and railings. Her world is gray, but she remembers colors and she dreams in color. For her ninth birthday, her father gives her a puzzle box and the Braille book, *Around the World in Eighty Days* by Jules Verne. She is delighted.

Key Happenings

- Marie-Laure can navigate the museum alone.

- Marie-Laure is enthralled by the book, *Around the World in Eighty Days*.

Chapter 18

Werner and Jutta improve the range on their radio and begin hearing programs from Verona, Dresden, and London. One night, they hear a children's science program in French.

Key Happenings

- Werner and Jutta extend the range of their radio.

- Werner is entranced by a children's science program narrated by a Frenchman.

Chapter 19

Marie-Laure hears rumors that the Sea of Flames is to be displayed. Although her father says rumors of the stone's curse are just stories, she hears other staff members whispering about it whenever anything goes wrong.

Her father has a secret project. Marie-Laure thinks he is building a display case for the stone.

Key Happenings

- Marie-Laure hears rumors that the Sea of Flames, a diamond thought to be cursed, will be displayed at the museum where her father works.

- Marie-Laure's father is working on a secret project. She believes he is building a display case for the Sea of Flames diamond.

Chapter 20

Werner and Jutta listen to the Frenchman's science broadcasts. Werner wants to become a scientist, not a miner.

Key Happenings

- Werner and Jutta listen to, and learn from, a children's science radio broadcast.

Chapter 21

The Sea of Flames is not displayed.

Marie-Laure's father begins taking her to work again. For her eleventh birthday, he gives her a wooden puzzle cube and a copy of part one of Jules Verne's *Twenty Thousand Leagues Under the Sea*.

Key Happenings

- The Sea of Flames diamond is not displayed at the museum where Marie-Laure's father works.

- Marie-Laure turns eleven. She receives part one of *Twenty Thousand Leagues Under the Sea* by Jules Verne.

Chapter 22

A Nazi official and his wife visit the orphanage. Werner is reading Hertz's *Principles of Mechanics.* The official takes the book, concerned it is inappropriate for a German child. Jutta brags that Werner is smart and will go to Berlin to study one day. The official declares Werner will work in the mines.

Key Happenings

- A visiting German official confiscates Werner's copy of *Principles of Mechanics.*

- A visiting German official tells Werner he will work in the mines no matter how smart he is.

Chapter 23

Marie-Laure hears rumors the Germans are preparing to invade Paris. Her father denies it, but, by the fall, she thinks she can smell gasoline under the wind, as if machines are steaming toward Paris.

Dr. Geffard teaches Marie-Laure about mollusk shells.

Key Happenings

- Paris is abuzz with rumors of a German invasion.

- Marie-Laure learns about mollusk shells from Dr. Geffard.

Chapter 24

Werner stays up late listening to the radio and studying math. He fixes and builds things, such as a machine to slice carrots. Everyone wants his services as a radio repairman.

Jutta worries when a girl is tossed out of the pool for being half-Jewish. Werner assures her the two of them are all German.

Key Happenings

- Werner becomes the neighborhood radio repairman.

- Jutta worries about being Jewish.

Chapter 25

In November 1939, some boys tell Marie-Laure the Germans do nasty things to blind girls. Her father continues to insist there will not be a war. Marie-Laure has nightmares about the Germans destroying the museum.

Jutta tries to send a letter to the professor who narrates the science program on the radio.

Key Happenings

- Marie-Laure is frightened by the idea of war.

Chapter 26

Werner turns fourteen in May, 1940. He fears being sent to the mines in a year. Everyone in town appears to be supportive of the Nazis.

Key Happenings

- Werner has nightmares of being sent to the mines.

Chapter 27

Marie's father works late as the museum sends its treasures away for safekeeping. Marie-Laure turns twelve, and her father gives her the second part of *Twenty Thousand Leagues Under the Sea*. On June 1, she hears planes. The radio goes silent.

Key Happenings

- Marie-Laure turns twelve and her birthday gift is the second part of *Twenty Thousand Leagues Under the Sea.*

- On June 1, Marie-Laure's radio goes silent as she hears planes flying overhead.

Chapter 28

It is dangerous to do so, but Jutta still listens to the radio. She tells Werner the Germans are bombing Paris.

Key Happenings

- Jutta learns from the radio that the Germans are bombing Paris.

Chapter 29

Marie-Laure and her father prepare to leave Paris as Germany invades. While walking to a train station, they hear that French forces are falling to the Germans. The city goes dark.

Key Happenings

- Marie-Laure and her father attempt to flee Paris by train.

Chapter 30

Rudolf Siedler, who runs the mines, needs a radio repaired. He has heard that Werner can do such work and sends someone to retrieve him. Siedler is so impressed when Werner repairs the radio, he promises to recommend Werner for an elite school. Back at the orphanage, Werner smashes his and Jutta's forbidden shortwave radio.

Key Happenings

- Werner is able to fix the mine commandant's radio.

- The commandant promises to recommend him to a prestigious school.

- Back home, Werner smashes the forbidden shortwave radio.

Chapter 31

There are no trains. Marie-Laure and her father walk. The museum director has a friend in Evreux who can help them, or they will go to the home of her father's uncle, Etienne, in Saint-Malo.

Marie-Laure's father opens his rucksack and takes out a hidden pouch that contains a blue gemstone that looks like the Sea of Flames. There are four, three decoys and the real one. A geologist has one, the museum security director another, one is at the museum, and this one. No one knows which is real.

Key Happenings

- Marie-Laure and her father must walk from Paris because there are no trains. They head to Evreux to see a friend of the museum director or, if he cannot help, to Saint-Malo where her great uncle, Etienne, lives.

- Marie-Laure's father is carrying a hidden stone that may be the Sea of Flames, or may be one of three replicas.

Part Two

Chapter 32

The bombers have come and gone. Most of the town is burning. The Hotel of Bees crumbles.

Key Happenings

- Saint-Malo burns after the bombing by the Americans. The Hotel of Bees, where Werner took refuge in the cellar, collapses.

Chapter 33

Marie-Laure huddles under her bed. Debris rains on her, but the house is standing.

Key Happenings

- Marie-Laure and Etienne's house survives the bombing of Saint-Malo and the resulting fire.

Chapter 34

Werner wakes in the collapsed cellar of the Hotel of Bees.

Key Happenings

- The cellar under the Hotel of Bees collapsed on top of Werner and his companions. Werner is trapped with Bernd and Volkheimer.

Chapter 35

Marie-Laure makes her way down to the cellar as more bombs explode in the city outside the house. She takes the model house with her.

Key Happenings

- Marie-Laure takes refuge in the cellar of Etienne's house.

Chapter 36

Werner sees a light, but it is not rescuers. It is Volkheimer's field light. The stairwell is destroyed and there is no other way out.

Key Happenings

- Werner and his companions cannot get out of the collapsed Hotel of Bees' cellar because the stairs are gone.

Part Three

Chapter 37

After two days of walking, Marie-Laure and her father reach their destination, but the museum director's friend has fled. They continue on to Saint-Malo and Uncle Etienne's home.

Key Happenings

- Marie-Laure and her father reach the home of the museum director's friend, but he has fled. They continue to Saint-Malo.

Chapter 38

Werner goes to Essen for eight days of entrance exams for the National Political Institutes of

Education. He fears he will fail. When the recruits are required to climb a ladder twenty-five feet and dive onto a flag held by other recruits, the first boy breaks his arms. Werner makes a clean jump.

Key Happenings

- Werner is tested over eight days of admission exams in Essen for the National Political Institutes of Education.

Chapter 39

Marie-Laure and her father get a ride on a truck that brings them close to Saint-Malo. They walk the rest of the way to the home of Uncle Etienne.

Key Happenings

- Marie-Laure and her father arrive at her great-uncle's home in Saint-Malo.

Chapter 40

Madame Manec, Uncle Etienne's elderly housekeeper, welcomes enthusiastically Marie-Laure and her father. Madame, as she is called, tells Marie-Laure's father that Etienne has been shut up inside the house for twenty years.

Key Happenings

- Uncle Etienne's housekeeper welcomes Marie-Laure and her father to his home in Saint-Malo.

Chapter 41

Werner is a celebrity back home when he is accepted to the National Political Institute of Education #6 at Schulpforta in Saxony. The whole area celebrates. Werner represents the hopes of the town, except for Jutta who is unhappy.

Key Happenings

- Werner is accepted to Schulpforta, a prestigious school. All of Zollverein, the town where the orphanage Werner lives in is, celebrates.

Chapter 42

Marie-Laure asks about Etienne. She learns he has not gone out since the Great War. She asks what occupation means and her father explains that it is military rule.

Key Happenings

- Marie-Laure learns more about Etienne and military occupation.

Chapter 43

Werner does not understand why Jutta is not happy for him. She tells him she has heard on the forbidden broadcasts that Germany is committing atrocities and the people are being lied to. She fears he will become a thug at school. She tells him he can lie to himself, but not to her.

Key Happenings

- Jutta tells Werner that Germans are committing atrocities and their leaders are lying to the people.

Chapter 44

Marie-Laure finds Uncle Etienne's private rooms where they talk about his radios and books. About the same time, her father goes into town just as the town leaders surrender to the Germans.

Key Happenings

- Marie-Laure meets Uncle Etienne.

- Marie-Laure's father witnesses the German takeover of Saint-Malo.

Chapter 45

The rules at Werner's new school are strict. The four hundred boys are told they will "eat country and breathe nation" (Jungmänner, EPUB).

Werner's bunkmate, Frederick, is from Berlin. Many of the students are rich, even noble. Werner is eager to fit in.

Key Happenings

- Werner is indoctrinated in his new school.

Chapter 46

Sergeant Major Reinhold von Rumpel, a gemologist from Stuttgart, appraises and tracks treasures for the Reich. He is seeking a diamond known as the Sea of Flames.

Key Happenings

- Nazi gemologist, Reinhold von Rumpel, is searching for the Sea of Flames.

Chapter 47

Marie-Laure's father tells the neighbors what he saw during the German takeover. There is now a curfew.

Marie-Laure and her father share a small room at Uncle Etienne's. They must stay there until he hears from Paris.

Key Happenings

- Marie-Laure's father tells her they cannot go back to Paris.

Chapter 48

The technical sciences teacher, Dr. Hauptmann, is impressed with Werner's mechanical skills.

Key Happenings

- Werner's mechanical skills come to the attention of science teacher, Dr. Hauptmann.

Chapter 49

The Bretons must surrender all weapons. Marie-Laure's father is making her a model of Saint-Malo. Etienne reads Darwin to her. She and Etienne play at being adventurers.

Key Happenings

- Uncle Etienne reads Darwin to Marie-Laure and plays games with her.

- Marie-Laure's father makes her a model of Saint-Malo.

Chapter 50

Hauptmann tests Werner in trigonometry and triangulation. The professor says Werner is to work in his lab every evening. He introduces Frank Volkheimer, an upperclassman, to Werner and tells him Volkheimer will be his protector against the other students.

Key Happenings

- Werner is assigned to work in Hauptmann's lab each evening.

Chapter 51

Uncle Etienne shows Marie-Laure a trapdoor under the kitchen table that leads to the cellar. She asks about a locked door in a sixth-floor bedroom. It leads to the garret. Marie-Laure sees there is machinery all over the garret when Etienne takes her there. Etienne puts a headset on Marie-Laure and she hears music, then a man giving a science lesson. Etienne explains that he and his brother, Henri, made the programs, with Henri narrating. Then the Great War came, and they became signalmen. Henri would whisper the scripts to him when he was terrified by light flares at night, but Henri died. After the war, Etienne built the massive transmitter and began broadcasting the programs and music, to try to reach his lost brother and bring him peace.

Werner writes three letters to Jutta that are censored. In the first, he describes his work with Hauptmann. In the second, he relates the tale of a captured German soldier. In the third he talks of Frederick, who "sees what other people don't" (The Professor, EPUB).

Key Happenings

- Etienne explains to Marie-Laure about the trap door hiding the cellar. When she asks about a door in the sixth floor bedroom, he takes her to the garret.

- Etienne allows Marie-Laure hear a program he transmits on his huge transmitter. He explains that he and his brother Henri wrote and recorded science programs for children.

Chapter 52

Claude Levitte, a struggling perfumer in Saint-Malo and now a meat smuggler, wants to score points with the Germans. He sees Marie-Laure's father making measurements and sketches in the streets. He plans to tell the German soldiers.

Key Happenings

- Perfumer Claude Levitte sees Marie-Laure's father making sketches and measurements on the street and plans to turn him in.

Chapter 53: Time of the Ostriches

Madame's friends tell horror stories of what is going on during the occupation. Madame does what she can to feed sick or stranded people.

Key Happenings

- Madame tries to aid those in need.

Chapter 54

Bastian, a sadistic officer in charge of field exercises at Werner's school, forces the weakest boy, Ernst, to run ahead of the pack of boys. If he reaches Bastian before the pack gets him, he will be safe. If not, he will be beaten. Though Ernst escapes, Werner is angry at the game. Yet, wonders if some part of him wants to see a beating.

Key Happenings

- An officer at Werner's school forces the boys to participate in a savage exercise in which a boy, chosen for being weak, must run to escape a beating.

- Werner wonders if some part of him wanted to see a weak boy in his class receive a beating for running too slow.

Chapter 55

All radios must be turned in by German command. Marie-Laure's father and Madame collect radios around Etienne's house, but do not to know about the transmitter in the garret.

Key Happenings

- All the radios in Etienne's house are relinquished to the Germans by command, except the transmitter in the garret.

Chapter 56

Von Rumpel's trail leads to the Paris museum. He asks about the Sea of Flames. When museum officials deny its existence, Von Rumpel threatens their children. They produce the blue stone.

Key Happenings

- Von Rumpel coerces museum officials to give him the Sea of Flames by threatening their children.

Chapter 57

Marie-Laure tells Etienne that his other radios have been turned in. He and Marie-Laure use a wheeled auto jack to push a huge wardrobe in front of the garret door.

Key Happenings

- Etienne and Marie-Laure use a big wardrobe to conceal access to the garret.

Chapter 58

Hauptmann tells Werner to boost the function of the directional radio receiver to measure the angle of transmissions. Volkheimer surprises Werner with his fondness for classical music. Frederick is struggling in school and not getting along with the other students. Werner tries to help him.

Key Happenings

- Werner is ordered to make a radio track the angle of transmission it is receiving.

- Frederick is floundering at school. Werner tries to help him.

Chapter 59

Marie-Laure's dad receives a telegram telling him to return to Paris.

Marie-Laure's father worries that the stone he carries is real. If so, Marie-Laure and, possibly, all of France are endangered because he carries it. He fears the telegram requesting him to return to Paris may be fake, but buys a train ticket anyway. At the station he locks eyes with Etienne's neighbor, the perfumer, and fears a betrayal. He gives Marie-Laure lots of soap for a bath, then tells her he must return to Paris. He promises to be back within ten days.

Key Happenings

- Marie-Laure's father buys a ticket for Paris even though he fears that the telegram requesting his return is fake.

Chapter 60

Officers come regularly to the school to tell boys their fathers have died in battle.

One day Frederick is weakest in Bastian's cruel game. The boys beat him with the commandant's rubber hose. Werner does nothing. Frederick takes the beating and gets back up.

Key Happenings

- Frederick is singled out as the weakest. He is beaten, but gets back up.

- Werner does nothing to help Frederick when he is beaten for being weak.

Chapter 61

Daniel LeBlanc, Marie-Laure's father, is arrested hours from Paris and quizzed about his sketches, tool case and keys. He is suspected of terrorism and arrested. After four days, he is taken east with other prisoners.

Key Happenings

- Daniel LeBlanc is arrested and taken east.

Part Four

Chapter 62

Von Rumpel watches the bombardment of Saint-Malo from a turret in the Fort of La Cite. He can see Etienne's house with binoculars.

Key Happenings

- Von Rumpel arrives at Saint-Malo.

Chapter 63

Werner's radio is a complete loss, as is the hearing in his left ear. Volkheimer hacks at the rubble. Werner thinks the three of them may be paying for their crimes against humanity.

Key Happenings

- Werner's radio is not working.

- Werner is deaf in his left ear.

- Volkheimer hacks at the rubble, but he and Werner are still trapped in the collapsed cellar of the Hotel of Bees.

Chapter 64

Marie-Laure awakens in the cellar and hears no sirens. She eats the last bit of bread, then finds two small cans of food. She cannot tell what is inside. She pockets the cans and waits for Etienne.

Key Happenings

- Marie-Laure and the house survive another night.

- She finds two cans of food.

- She continues to wait for Etienne.

Chapter 65

The shelling ceases again at six p.m. Von Rumpel, carrying his pistol, water and morphine, goes to Etienne's house. He finds it nearly intact.

Key Happenings

- Von Rumpel arrives at Etienne's house.

Chapter 66

Werner does not know if it is day or night. Volkheimer tries to nurse Bernd. They have three rations and two canteens of water, two grenades and a rifle with five rounds. Werner knows they need only three, one for each man. He feels as if he is trapped in the mines after all.

Key Happenings

- Werner, Volkheimer and Bernd are still trapped and low on food and water.

Chapter 67

As Marie-Laure is upstairs attempting to open one of the food cans, a trip wire left to warn of intruders goes off. Someone comes in the house.

Key Happenings

- Marie-Laure is on the third floor of Etienne's house when a trip wire goes off and alerts her that someone has entered the

house.

Part Five

Chapter 68

Frederick invites Werner to his home in Berlin for school break. Werner is amazed by the family's possessions. Frederick is most proud of two volumes of Audubon's bird drawings, a banned book.

Frederick confesses to Werner that he has bad vision. His binoculars are prescription and he memorized charts to pass the eye exam for school.

Frederick's mother tells a woman the Jewess on the top floor of their building will be gone soon, freeing up her apartment. Werner feels uneasy.

Frederick tells him their lives are not their own anymore.

Key Happenings

- Werner visits Frederick's home in Berlin and is amazed at the family's riches. However, he is bothered by discussions of a Jewish woman who lives on the top floor.

- Frederick reveals he is hiding his poor vision from the school.

- Frederick shows Werner his precious, but banned, Audubon books.

Chapter 69

Marie-Laure is angry and depressed after twenty days without word from her father. The museum says he never arrived.

Key Happenings

- Daniel LeBlanc has disappeared.

Chapter 70

Bastian has a prisoner staked in the schoolyard. He tells the boys the barbarian would tear out their throats if freed, then turns them loose with buckets of water to throw on the man in the freezing weather. Werner wants to flee, but throws his water anyway. Frederick finally stops the torture of the prisoner by refusing to dump his bucket.

Key Happenings

- Bastian orders the boys at Werner's school torture a prisoner by dumping water on him in the cold.

- Werner is upset but does as he is told.

- Frederick refuses to toss water on a freezing prisoner at Bastian's command.

Chapter 71

Twenty-nine days after her father disappeared, Madame takes Marie-Laure out to the ocean.

Key Happenings

- Marie-Laure goes to the ocean.

Chapter 72

Von Rumpel is back in Paris seeking the Sea of Flames. The museum's copy was a fake. He has the lapidary who made the fake, Dupont, arrested.

Marie-Laure's father writes that he is working in Germany.

Key Happenings

- Von Rumpel knows the Sea of Flames given to him at the Paris museum is fake.

- Von Rumpel has arrested the lapidary who made the fake Sea of Flames for the museum.

- A letter comes from Daniel informing his family he is working Germany.

Chapter 73

The dead prisoner remains in the courtyard with crows pecking at him until the custodian takes the corpse away. Frederick is bullied and chosen three times as the weakest in nine days. Werner tries to lose himself in lab work. The boys are taught about entropy and how the Nazis are bringing order to the evolution of humanity.

Key Happenings

- Frederick is being bullied while Werner continues to do nothing to help him.

Chapter 74

Madame takes Marie-Laure daily to the ocean, the market, and the butcher. They bring food to those in need, including World War I veteran, Harold Bazin.

Key Happenings

- Marie-Laure settles in at Saint-Malo now that she can go out, especially to the ocean.

- Marie-Laure helps Madame take food to those in need.

Chapter 75

Werner's radio triangulation device, the one he has built at Hauptmann's instruction, works in test runs with Volkheimer as the target. Once Werner thinks Hauptmann means to shoot Volkheimer, but the professor fires into the sky. He is merely teaching them that a soldier cannot hesitate in battle.

Key Happenings

- Werner's triangulation device works.

- Professor Hauptmann teaches Werner and Volkheimer that a soldier cannot hesitate in battle.

Chapter 76

Madame urges her lady friends to stop just complaining about the occupation and take action by doing simple things to hamper the Germans.

Key Happenings

- Madame proposes her friends do little things to hamper the occupation.

Chapter 77

The bullying of Frederick intensifies. Werner tells Frederick he could just go home. Frederick responds that they should not be friends anymore.

Key Happenings

- The bullying of Frederick drives a wedge between him and Werner.

Chapter 78

The ladies of Madame's resistance club, rearrange road signs and misprint train schedules. They

divert a rayon shipment to the wrong address.
They write freedom slogans on banknotes.

Key Happenings

- Madame and her friends begin a campaign
  of nuisance against the Germans.

Chapter 79

Von Rumpel thinks about all the treasures the
Germans are collecting and how he will someday
visit Hitler's great museum in Linz to see his own
contribution, the Sea of Flames. He did not get
names from Dupont, but did get a lead.

Key Happenings

- Von Rumpel continues to look for the Sea of Flames.

Chapter 80

One April morning Frederick is gone. The school nurse tells Werner Frederick was taken to Leipzig for surgery. Werner never learns what happened.

Key Happenings

- Frederick leaves school to have surgery. Werner never learns what happened to him.

Chapter 81

Another smuggled letter comes from Daniel. He does not say where, but he is building a road and is safe. He asks them to keep sending packages. He hopes one will get through.

Harold Bazin opens a locked gate and takes Madame and Marie-Laure to see a low grotto, once used as a kennel for guard dogs, beneath the city walls. It is a snail heaven. Harold gives Marie-Laure a key to it.

Key Happenings

- Harold Bazin reveals a snail-filled grotto to Madame and Marie-Laure. He gives Marie-Laure a key to it.

- Another letter gets through from Daniel. Marie-Laure and Etienne believe he may be working in Germany.

Chapter 82

Werner learns Frederick has brain damage.

The boys are told of victories on the Russian front. Volkheimer goes to war. New boys come, intoxicated with fear and fervor.

Werner misses Jutta, especially her sense of right and wrong. The transceiver Werner built is being produced in Berlin. Werner sits in the lab late at night, searching radio broadcasts for something he cannot name.

Key Happenings

- Frederick is brain damaged.

- Volkheimer goes to war.

- The transceiver Werner built is produced in Berlin for use in the field.

Chapter 83

Madame and her friends are approached by a man from the resistance who asks if they can track ships.

Werner receives a letter from Jutta. She sends along a notebook of Werner's boyhood drawings and inventions.

Key Happenings

- The resistance recruits the old ladies to spy on the Germans.

- Jutta sends Werner his notebook of drawings.

Chapter 84

Madame asks Etienne to transmit numerical radio messages for the resistance. He refuses, stating he does not want to endanger Marie-Laure.

Key Happenings

- Etienne refuses to help the resistance out of fear of placing Marie-Laure in danger.

Chapter 85

Werner asks Dr. Hauptmann if he can be sent home. The professor grows angry and halts Werner's special treatment.

- Dr. Hauptmann denies Werner's request to leave school.

Chapter 86

Harold is gone. Only half the ladies come to the next meeting. They think Harold might have been carrying messages for the resistance in the baked bread he delivered and fear for themselves. They decide to take a break.

Key Happenings

- Harold Bazin disappears. He may have been carrying messages for the resistance.

- The ladies decide to take a break in their activities against the Germans out of fear of arrest.

Chapter 87

Instructors vanish at the school. Broken old men replace them. Lights and power are erratic and the food is rotten. More fathers die. Yet all the war news is good. Hauptmann is rewarded for his work and called to Berlin.

Key Happenings

- Werner's school is running low on everything but good news about the war.

- Hauptmann goes to work in Berlin in response to Werner's work on the transceiver.

Chapter 88

French police come to Etienne's house, supposedly at the museum's request. Daniel has been convicted of theft and conspiracy. He was sent to a labor camp, maybe Breitenau. The museum cannot help. The police would like to see any letters from him. They search the house and find three Free French flags, but do nothing. Etienne burns the flags.

Key Happenings

- French police tell Etienne and Marie-Laure that Daniel has been convicted of theft and conspiracy. He is likely at Breitenau, a labor camp.

- The French police read Daniel's letters and search Etienne's house, but leave.

Chapter 89

Madame has been disappearing more. She argues with Etienne about the resistance.

Key Happenings

- Madame is gone more and more, likely working for the resistance.

Chapter 90

Werner is told that he has been lying about his age and must join the Wehrmacht, the German military, immediately. It is not true, but he agrees.

Key Happenings

- The commandant of the school makes it appear that Werner has been lying about his age and forces him to join the Wehrmacht immediately.

Chapter 91

Damp fog rises in the spring and Madame gets pneumonia. Etienne nurses her.

In a letter to Marie-Laure, Daniel says he has received two parcels and has been allowed to keep a comb and a toothbrush. He tells his daughter to look in the model of Etienne's house to understand his disappearance.

Key Happenings

- Madame has pneumonia.

- Daniel writes to Marie-Laure. The letter suggests the model of Etienne's house is important to her understanding of his disappearance.

Chapter 92

Von Rumpel, diagnosed with cancer, is weak and dizzy from his treatments. He studies the Sea of Flames. He thinks about the curse, how the keeper of the stone is said to live forever.

Key Happenings

- Von Rumpel is ill, but still pursuing the Sea of Flames.

Chapter 93

Madame is somewhat better after her bout with pneumonia. She promises she will not work with the resistance, but when Marie-Laure goes out with her she is certain Madame exchanged envelopes with a woman on the street.

Key Happenings

- Madame is recovering from pneumonia. It does not stop her from getting back to resistance work.

Chapter 94

Werner goes to Berlin to see Frederick. The family has moved to the old Jewish woman's apartment. Frederick does not know Werner and scribbles spirals on paper all day long. The family denies ever having Frederick's favorite Audubon books.

Key Happenings

- Werner visits Frederick. The family now lives in the old Jewish woman's larger apartment.

- Frederick is profoundly brain damaged.

Chapter 95

Madame becomes ill again and dies.

Key Happenings

- Madame dies.

Part Six

Chapter 96

Marie-Laure can hear an intruder. She recognizes the limp of the sergeant major with the dead voice. She goes through the wardrobe and hides in the garret.

Key Happenings

- Marie-Laure hears the intruder in the house and recognizes the limp of the German sergeant major. She makes it safely through the wardrobe into the garret.

Chapter 97

Bernd dies. Werner tries to get the radio to work.

Key Happenings

- Walter Bernd dies of his injuries.

Chapter 98

Von Rumpel searches Etienne's house. He passes by the wardrobe, then finds the wooden model of the town. He thinks the Sea of Flames must be inside it.

Key Happenings

- Von Rumpel searches the house and finds the model of Saint-Malo. He thinks the Sea of Flames is hidden inside the model.

Chapter 99

Werner tries to piece together the radio, but only succeeds in receiving static.

Key Happenings

- Werner tries to get the radio working again.

Chapter 100

Marie-Laure climbs to the very top of the attic. A shell flies past. She waits but she knows the German will not leave.

Key Happenings

- Marie-Laure goes to the top of the attic to hide.

Part Seven

Chapter 101

Werner's Wehrmacht unit consists of Neumann One, the driver; Neumann Two, a corporal; an engineer; a sergeant, and Werner. Neumann Two comes on foot to collect Werner. They take a train and get off near Lodz. Werner sees trains full of prisoners sitting on the bodies of dead prisoners.

Key Happenings

- Neumann Two, a corporal from Werner's new unit, arrives to take him to his new unit.

Chapter 102

Etienne holes up in his room to mourn Madame. When he emerges, he is determined to carry on her work by making the number broadcasts, the reading of important numbers over his radio, she had asked him to do before. The messages will be put into bread from the bakery that Marie-Laure will pick up.

Key Happenings

- Etienne decides to make the number broadcasts, with Marie-Laure's help.

  Messages will come in bread from the bakery.

Chapter 103

Werner arrives in a devastated Russia. Werner is to work in a three-ton radio truck. The truck carries two of the transceivers Werner designed. Volkheimer appears.

Key Happenings

- Werner arrives in Russia and takes up his station in a radio truck.

- Volkheimer turns up in Russia.

Chapter 104

Marie-Laure brings home the first set of numbers. Etienne thinks they may be frequencies, plus a time. After dark the numbers go flying out.

Key Happenings

- Etienne and Marie-Laure make their first transmission of numbers.

Chapter 105

Volkheimer is Werner's sergeant. Werner also meets the engineer, Walter Bernd, and gap-toothed Neumann One. Volkheimer tells Werner that partisans are attacking trains and they need working transceivers. Werner fixes the equipment quickly.

Key Happenings

- Werner learns Volkheimer is his sergeant.

- Werner repairs the transceivers.

Chapter 106

Etienne has been broadcasting the numbers for several months. His ghosts, the memories of people from his past that have been haunting him, are gone. He adds bits of music to the transmissions.

Key Happenings

- Etienne has been broadcasting number for the resistance for months. It helps him deal with his past.

Chapter 107

Werner and his crew drive through fields of fading sunflowers in the Ukraine. They track a transmission to a cottage. Neumann One and Volkheimer kill the partisans. Volkheimer tells them to grab the radio equipment and burn the cottage. Werner disapproves of the haphazard equipment, as though it is a disgrace to the magic of radio.

Key Happenings

- Werner and his new unit make their first kill using the transceivers.

Chapter 108

Von Rumpel gets a summons to a warehouse near Lodz. Thousands of jewels taken from prisoners must be pried out of their settings, cleaned and tallied.

Key Happenings

- Von Rumpel assesses a hoard of jewelry taken from prisoners.

Chapter 109

Marie-Laure gets ready for her day. Some days the bread holds a scroll, but not always. She goes to the grotto to tend to the snails. It has been a year since Harold gave her the key. At home, the power fails often and they are burning anything, even antiques, to stay warm.

Key Happenings

- Marie-Laure has settled into a routine of going to the bakery and the grotto to tend the snails.

Chapter 110

By January 1943, Werner's unit is regularly finding illegal transmissions. Their success thrills their captain, who promises them leave, steaks, and brandy.

Key Happenings

- Werner's unit is highly successful at finding and eliminating partisans radio signals.

Chapter 111

In summer 1943, the baker's wife, Madame Ruelle, asks Etienne to read personal messages on his broadcasts in order to connect with those who have fled Saint-Malo.

Key Happenings

- Etienne adds personal news to the resistance broadcasts.

Chapter 112

Von Rumpel goes to the Pyrenees to check out another Sea of Flames, but it is another fake.

Key Happenings

- Von Rumpel finds a second fake Sea of Flames.

Chapter 113

In December 1943, Marie-Laure still makes her rounds to the bakery. Her vibrant inner world of Paris has turned into the gray of wartime Saint-

Malo. Only her uncle's broadcasts bring color to the world.

Key Happenings

- Etienne's broadcasts continue into December 1943.

Chapter 114

Werner becomes ill as 1944 begins. While his unit continues to hunt partisans, he sees a threat in anyone who is not German.

Key Happenings

- Werner is ill. His unit continues to find partisan radio signals.

Chapter 115

Von Rumpel takes a third Sea of Flames from the safe of a retired paleontologist, but it is fake.

Key Happenings

- Von Rumpel locates the third fake Sea of Flames.

Chapter 116

Partisans blow up a German truck on a bridge south of Saint-Malo. The Germans blame the attack on resistance radio broadcasts. All able-bodied men are required to work on fortifying the Atlantic wall, the wall along the side of the city that borders on the Atlantic Ocean.

Key Happenings

- Germans blame a partisan attack on the resistance radio network.

Chapter 117

Von Rumpel's trail leads to Daniel's Paris flat. He finds the model of the neighborhood, Marie-Laure's clothes, and Braille books in her room, allowing him to believe she is blind.

Key Happenings

- Von Rumpel suspects Daniel LeBlanc has the Sea of Flames, but does not find it in his Paris flat.

- He deducts that LeBlanc's daughter is blind.

Chapter 118

In April 1944, Werner's unit works in Vienna. His fever returns. The sight of a little girl in a maroon cape playing lifts Werner's spirits but the child is killed by Neumann Two when a transmission leads to her apartment. They find no radio.

Key Happenings

- Werner's illness returns.

- A raid goes wrong. Neumann Two kills a woman and a little girl whose existence cheered Werner earlier in the day.

Chapter 119

For her sixteenth birthday, Etienne surprises Marie-Laure with a new copy of *Twenty*

Thousand Leagues Under the Sea. She reads it to Etienne.

Key Happenings

- Etienne gives Marie-Laure a new copy of *Twenty Thousand Leagues Under the Sea* for her sixteenth birthday.

Chapter 120

A new German commander arrives in Saint-Malo. He sends a telegram to Berlin, requesting a unit to locate and take down a partisan radio network.

Key Happenings

- The new Saint-Malo commander requests help locating and destroying a network of terrorist broadcasts.

Part Eight

Chapter 121

Three days into the siege, it is finally quiet in Saint-Malo, though fires burn everywhere. An American shell hits Fort National, killing nine French prisoners.

Key Happenings

- An American shell kills nine French prisoners at Fort National.

Chapter 122

Marie-Laure, hiding in the garret, hears the German urinating into the sixth-floor toilet. He makes such a noise, she believes him to be ill. She opens a can of green beans with her brick, timing the noise so the explosions outside mask it.

Key Happenings

- Marie-Laure, starving, opens a can of green beans by timing the sound with explosions outside to prevent tipping off the German to her presence.

Chapter 123

Werner still has not fixed the radio. He and Volkheimer discuss whether they should try to blast out of the collapsed building with the grenades.

Key Happenings

- Werner's radio still does not work.

Chapter 124

Von Rumpel battles visions, sweats profusely, and tastes blood, but will not give up. He starts to search the house again.

Key Happenings

- Although very ill, Von Rumpel keeps searching Etienne's house for the Sea of Flames.

Chapter 125

The sound of falling rain makes Marie-Laure realize she needs water. She creeps downstairs to drink from a bucket. She can smell and hear the

German below. She realizes she cannot get past him to return to the cellar and goes back to the garret.

Key Happenings

- Marie-Laure manages to get a drink of water despite the German's presence in the house. She then retreats back to the garret.

Chapter 126

Volkheimer talks about his great-grandfather, who made masts for ships from giant trees. Werner contrasts this to his town, where they dug up prehistoric trees in mines.

Key Happenings

- Volkheimer and Werner talk about home and family.

Chapter 127

Marie-Laure manages to switch on the transmitter and begins to read her book aloud. Perhaps Etienne is alive and will hear it.

Key Happenings

- Marie-Laure reads *Twenty Thousand Leagues Under the Sea* over Etienne's radio transmitter.

Chapter 128

Werner hears Marie-Laure reading on the radio, which now works some of the time. She says someone is in her house. Werner knows he must save her.

Key Happenings

- Werner's radio works. He hears Marie-Laure and wants to save her.

Part Nine

Chapter 129

The girl in the velvet, maroon cape haunts Werner as he reads Jutta's letter, detailing how Herr Siedler praises him. His unit arrives in Saint-Malo to help locate the resistance radio network. Werner goes to the ocean. Bernd yells to him that the beach has been mined.

Key Happenings

- Werner's unit arrives in Saint-Malo to locate the resistance radio network.

Chapter 130

A doctor in Nuremberg gives Von Rumpel three or four months to live. A call comes from France with information about Daniel LeBlanc that leads to the informer Claude Levitte in Saint-Malo.

Key Happenings

- Von Rumpel learns he will die soon of his cancer.

- A call leads Von Rumpel to Saint-Malo in his search for the Sea of Flames.

Chapter 131

Spring blooms in the last days of May 1944. The baker's wife gives Marie-Laure a special message for Etienne. The allies are coming. This confirms rumors Etienne has been hearing on the radio for weeks.

Key Happenings

- D-Day is about to take place. The resistance hopes this will lead to the liberation of France.

Chapter 132

Werner and his unit search day and night, but the transmissions have gone dead. The dead girl still haunts Werner. Werner writes to his sister that he has recovered. He tells her how much he loves the sea.

Key Happenings

- Werner's unit cannot find the partisan network.

Chapter 133

Finally Werner picks up the broadcast they are seeking. He realizes the voice is the one he heard on the children's science program so long ago. He thinks of Frederick dumping the pail of water, then tells Volkheimer he has heard nothing.

Key Happenings

- Werner picks up the broadcasts his unit has been waiting for in order to locate the resistance radio network. However, he recognizes the science professor's voice and decides not to tell Volkheimer.

Chapter 134

Eight Austrian airmen move into the Hotel of Bees and fortify it with an antiaircraft gun. Werner realizes the partisans are using a chimney to mount their antenna. He locates it at Number 4 rue Vauborel.

Key Happenings

- Werner finds the antenna of the resistance's radio network on Etienne's house.

Chapter 135

Levitte the perfumer identifies Etienne's house to Von Rumpel as the place where Daniel LeBlanc stayed.

Key Happenings

- The perfumer leads Von Rumpel to Etienne's house.

Chapter 136

Werner approaches Etienne's house. A pretty girl comes out. She has glasses and a cane, suggesting she is blind. He follows her to a bakery. A sallow German sergeant major sits on a bench nearby. The girl leaves the bakery and comes so close to Werner he can count her freckles.

Key Happenings

- Werner goes to Etienne's house and follows Marie-Laure to the bakery.

- A German sits on a bench near the bakery when Marie-Laure goes to pick up the day's bread.

Chapter 137

Marie-Laure goes to the grotto. As she exits, a man with rot in his breath, Von Rumpel, greets her in German-accented French. He asks about her father. She retreats, hoping he cannot follow. She can hear him pacing outside. He has a distinctive limp.

Key Happenings

- Von Rumpel follows Marie-Laure to the grotto and questions her. She manages to get inside.

- Marie-Laure can hear that Von Rumpel has a distinctive limp.

Chapter 138

When Marie-Laure is late returning from her errands, Etienne overcomes his fear of going outside and searches for her.

Key Happenings

- Etienne searches for Marie-Laure when she is later returning from her errands.

Chapter 139

Von Rumpel badgers Marie-Laure from outside the grotto. She angrily tells him her father left her only a model of the town. He seems convinced.

Key Happenings

- Marie-Laure tells Von Rumpel that her father left her nothing but a model of the town when he was arrested.

Chapter 140

Etienne finds Marie-Laure in the grotto.

Key Happenings

- Etienne finds Marie-Laure safe at the grotto.

Chapter 141

Werner thinks of the blind girl as they search for the radio network. Her memory replaces his dark visions of the dead child. A broadcast is expected and Werner plans to cover it up.

Key Happenings

- Werner plots to hide evidence of the next resistance broadcast.

Chapter 142

Etienne begins to go to the bakery in Marie-Laure's place. Von Rumpel comes to ask Etienne whether Daniel left something behind that belonged to the museum. Marie-Laure realizes the item Von Rumpel is searching for must be in the little house. She finds the Sea of Flames.

Key Happenings

- Etienne takes over the bakery runs.

- Von Rumpel visits Etienne, seeking an item from the museum.

- Marie-Laure finds the Sea of Flames inside the model of Etienne's house.

Chapter 143

Etienne agrees to find and broadcast the locations of three flak batteries. The baker's wife tells him that all able-bodied men will be interned at Fort National.

Key Happenings

- Etienne is to get the locations of flak batteries and broadcast them.

Chapter 144

Marie-Laure puts the diamond back in the little house, wondering if its curse has caused her sorrow. Etienne tells her at midnight that he must go out. She asks if he is sorry Daniel brought her. He responds she is the best thing in his life.

Key Happenings

- Marie-Laure puts the Sea of Flames back in the model of Etienne's house.

- Etienne goes out at midnight to make a special broadcast.

Chapter 145

Etienne broadcasts the location of one battery, but is arrested just before dawn by Von Rumpel.

Key Happenings

- Etienne is arrested.

Chapter 146

Etienne does not come home. Marie-Laure fills two buckets and the bathtub with water. Claude Levitte, the perfumer, tries to convince her to evacuate with him. He insists that Etienne sent him. Suspicious, she refuses and bolts the door.

Key Happenings

- Etienne is missing.

- Claude Levitte wants Marie-Laure to evacuate, but she refuses.

Chapter 147

Werner and his unit dine at the hotel. He goes atop to view the city and thinks of the girl, that he has protected her. He sees the glow of a distant battle and knows the Americans are coming. An airplane delivers leaflets. In the lobby, an Austrian looks at a copy. It is in French, a warning to evacuate.

Key Happenings

- Werner and the others at the Hotel of Bees find the leaflets warning French citizens to flee Saint-Malo.

Part Ten

Chapter 148

Werner hears the girl on the radio call for help. He confesses his deception about the transmitter to Volkheimer, who does not respond.

Key Happenings

- Werner admits his lies to Volkheimer as he continues to listen to the girl transmitting over the radio.

Chapter 149

Etienne survives the shell that falls on the fort. He watches the town burn.

Key Happenings

- Etienne is still alive in the fort.

Chapter 150

Marie-Laure is nearly done broadcasting the final chapters of *Twenty Thousand Leagues Under the Sea* by August 12. She hears nothing from the German. She considers giving him the Sea of Flames.

Key Happenings

- Marie-Laure considers breaking the curse by giving Von Rumpel the Sea of Flames.

Chapter 151

A German corporal comes to Etienne's house. Surprised to find Von Rumpel, he announces that the Germans are evacuating in advance of a cease-

fire the next day.

Key Happenings

- Von Rumpel still waits at Etienne's house.
  A German corporal tells him the Germans
  are leaving the city the following day.

Chapter 152

Werner hears the girl finish the story. The ground

quakes from the assault.

Key Happenings

- Werner continues to listen to Marie-Laure
  on the radio.

Chapter 153

Starving again, Marie-Laure plays loud music on Etienne's machines. She dares the German to come find her.

Key Happenings

- Marie-Laure plays loud music and waits for the German.

Chapter 154

Volkheimer hears "Clair de Lune" on the radio. He builds a makeshift bunker of rubble and blasts the grenades where the stairwell was.

Key Happenings

- Volkheimer explodes the grenades where the stairs were in hopes of creating an exit.

Chapter 155

Von Rumpel has visions of his little girls. He thinks he hears piano music. When it stops, he hears a man's voice talking about coal.

Key Happenings

- Von Rumpel thinks he is hallucinating, but he hears what Marie-Laure is broadcasting.

Chapter 156

The blast showers Volkheimer and Werner with debris, but opens a hole for their escape. Volkheimer gives Werner his rifle and tells him to go. Werner is determined to save Marie-Laure.

Key Happenings

- Werner and Volkheimer are free.

- Werner heads for Etienne's house.

Chapter 157

As Von Rumpel finds Marie-Laure's hiding place, someone comes in the house.

Key Happenings

- Von Rumpel figures out Marie-Laure is hiding behind the wardrobe.

- Someone comes into the house.

Chapter 158

Werner enters the house and climbs to the sixth floor. The sergeant major startles him, then tells him a ceasefire is coming. Von Rumpel thinks

Werner is after the Sea of Flames. He pulls his gun. Werner goes for his rifle.

Key Happenings

- Werner encounters Von Rumpel, who thinks Werner wants the Sea of Flames.

Chapter 159

Marie-Laure hears new footsteps in the house, then a shot. Volkheimer finds food. The Americans close in. Werner calls to Marie-Laure.

Key Happenings

- Marie-Laure hears a shot.

- Werner calls to Marie-Laure.

Chapter 160

Marie-Laure opens the wardrobe door and Werner

helps her out. Von Rumpel's body is in her bed.

Key Happenings

- Von Rumpel is dead.

- Marie-Laure and Werner meet.

Chapter 161

Marie-Laure and Werner talk. He reveals that he

heard the science broadcasts when he was a child.

She identifies the professor as her great-uncle.

They share a can of golden peaches.

Key Happenings

- Marie-Laure and Werner talk, then share a

  can of peaches.

Chapter 162

Marie-Laure shows Werner the transceiver and all of Etienne's books. One has Audubon reprints from which she lets him tear a page. Bombs fall and they hide in the cellar.

Key Happenings

- Marie-Laure and Werner take refuge in the cellar.

- He takes a page from an Audubon reprint book.

Chapter 163

The bombs stop. Marie-Laure takes Werner to the grotto, where she sets a small wooden item into the sea. He gives her a white pillowcase to wave and tells her she will be safer without him. She presses something into his hand and goes reluctantly. He finds the little iron key to the grotto in his hand.

Key Happenings

- Marie-Laure takes Werner to the grotto, where she puts a little wooden item in the sea. She then gives him the grotto key as they sadly part.

Chapter 164

Marie-Laure shelters in a school. She eats stacks of confiscated German chocolate. The commandant surrenders. The Americans free

Etienne, who finds Marie-Laure and takes her to Paris.

Key Happenings

- The town is liberated. Marie-Laure and Etienne find each other.

Chapter 165

French partisans capture Werner. On September 1, Werner is sent to a hospital tent. He is fevered and cannot keep food down. He wanders off and dies when he steps on a German land mine.

Key Happenings

- Werner is captured. Ill and delirious, he steps on a landmine and is killed.

Part Eleven

Chapter 166

Frau Elena and the last four girls at the orphanage, including Jutta, are living in Berlin, making machine parts. Jutta has been notified of Werner's death. Russian soldiers invade that May. Jutta is brutalized, but survives.

Key Happenings

- Jutta survives the war.

Chapter 167

Etienne and Marie-Laure move back into Daniel's old flat. Though Daniel is still missing, museum officials help Marie-Laure with housing and education. No one talks of the Sea of Flames.

Key Happenings

- Etienne and Marie-Laure move back to Paris.

Part Twelve

Chapter 168

A broken man, Volkheimer lives alone in Germany. He fixes and installs antennas. He receives a letter asking him to identify a dead soldier's belongings. They are Werner's.

Key Happenings

- Volkheimer identifies Werner's belongings.

Chapter 169

Jutta, now a math teacher, and her husband have a small son, Max, who is bright like Werner. Volkheimer delivers Werner's belongings to her.

He tells her Werner may have fallen in love in Saint-Malo.

Key Happenings

- Volkheimer brings Werner's belongings to Jutta.

Chapter 170

Jutta opens Werner's duffel. She finds a tiny model house, his old notebook, and a sealed envelope marked with Frederick's name.

Key Happenings

- Among Werner's belongings are a tiny wooden house, his notebook, and a letter for Frederick.

Chapter 171

Jutta takes Max to Saint-Malo, which has been rebuilt. At a museum, a man identifies the tiny model as the old LeBlanc house. He tells Jutta there was a girl in the house, a blind girl, whose address he can give her. Max figures out how to open the little house.

Key Happenings

- Jutta searches for the girl Volkheimer thought Werner might have fallen in love with in Saint-Malo.

Chapter 172

Marie-Laure is now a mollusk expert and works at the museum. All she knows of her father is that he was at a labor camp in 1943. She is stunned when Jutta and Max bring the tiny model house to her.

Key Happenings

- Marie-Laure is now a scientist in Paris.

- Jutta brings her the little model of Etienne's Saint-Malo house.

Chapter 173

Jutta tells Marie-Laure that Werner died. Marie-Laure recounts how he saved her life. She also tells Jutta that her great-uncle was the radio science professor. She will send Jutta the last existing recording, for Max.

Key Happenings

- Jutta tells Marie-Laure of Werner's death. Marie-Laure tells how he saved her life.

Chapter 174

Jutta calls home as Max soars a paper airplane over Paris. She has at last seen the city she imagined.

Key Happenings

- Jutta calls home after putting all the pieces together.

Chapter 175

Marie-Laure opens the wooden house. She wonders if Werner put the gem into the sea. The iron key pops out.

- Marie-Laure finds the iron key in the little box.

Chapter 176

The earth goes about its business, turning carbon into diamond.

Key Happenings

- New diamonds are made in the earth.

Chapter 177

Brain-damaged Frederick lives in a triplex with his mother in Berlin. Werner's letter comes. Inside is an Audubon print. His mother thinks maybe he is aware of it.

Key Happenings

- Werner's letter containing an Audubon print makes its way to Frederick, who now lives with his mother in Berlin.

Part Thirteen

Chapter 178

Marie-Laure and her grandson go to the park. He is almost twelve. He plays a hand-held video game. She thinks of the invisible electronic world around her. She wonders if the souls of lost loved ones travel those invisible paths.

Key Happenings

- Marie-Laure goes to the park with her grandson and muses on her losses.

A Reader's Perspective

A terrifying beauty fills the story of star-crossed teens Werner Pfennig and Marie-Laure LeBlanc. Every sentence, paragraph and page is polished like the diamond that the Nazi treasure hunter Von Rumpel seeks, though the horrors of World War II and the Third Reich emerge starkly. One passage, for example, evokes Picasso's classic painting *Guernica* with images of maddened horses running between burning cars and houses as a priest scatters holy water and Germans soldiers drink wine during the siege of Saint-Malo.

Such vivid images of war and suffering fill the novel. One of the main themes, however, is the ultimate triumph of light over darkness, and images of light shine through even in dark moments. One of the science lectures that Werner hears on the forbidden radio as a boy explains how the brain exists in darkness, but builds a world of light. The science professor is a LeBlanc, Marie-Laure's family name, which is French for "the white." When Werner first sees Marie-Laure, she is outlined in silver light. Marie-Laure becomes a symbol of purity, both for the reader and for Werner, who then realizes that he must save her.

Puzzles are another important theme in the novel. Marie-Laure's father Daniel LeBlanc makes them out of wood. Werner likes to solve them. Von Rumpel is obsessed by the puzzle of the diamond. Underlying these puzzles is the main one that the book raises: Why does evil happen?

The story is powerful, but by its very nature, this long novel is not an easy read, and its organization is its chief flaw. Though divided into 178 short chapters, the story threads often make confusing jumps in time. Sometimes the reader may have to flip back and forth to figure out, for example, how and when Marie-Laure learned that the German intruder terrorizing her in her uncle's home had a limp.

The characters, however, are so well crafted that they all come vibrantly alive, even those who have little time in the spotlight. The storylines are refreshing, too. It is much better for the novel that Werner and Marie-Laure do not become *Titanic*-style lovers, so that they stay real people. Neither has had a romance before, and they are quite young, so they are naturally shy. They also know they must put any dreams on hold.

There's also a hint of magical realism in the myth of the Sea of Flames diamond, which may, or may not, carry a real curse or drive even an industrious

Nazi like Van Rumpel over the edge. The war does end as the stone is cast away, so perhaps the curse is real.

The novel's main messages, despite its litany of the horrors of war and Nazi atrocities, are universal and hopeful: that goodness, more than anything else, abides and, no one should stop believing in it. The novel's very title sums it up: all the light is there, even when it cannot be seen. Yet despite the rescue of Marie-Laure, the symbol of goodness and purity, it still may be difficult for readers to fully accept the messages about faith and goodness. The puzzle still remains unsolved: why does such evil happen?

~~~~~~~~~~~~ END OF

SUMMARY~~~~~~~~~~~~

Thank you for purchasing this summary. We hope

you enjoyed it. If so,

please leave a review. We are interested in talking

to you to learn how we can improve! Please email

instaread.summaries@gmail.com with "Survey"

in the subject field to take a quick survey. We will

send you a $5 gift card from the store of your

choice upon completion of the survey! -:)

This is an unofficial summary. We encourage you to purchase the full book if you have not already. We will give you 10% off up to $1 on the digital version of the full-form book or $1 off on the physical version of the full-form book. Simply email instaread.summaries@gmail.com with "Discount for All The Light We Cannot See." in the subject field. Also include from which online book store you would like the discount and you can mention it in the subject or in the body of the email.

Made in the USA
Lexington, KY
22 October 2014